FALSE PROPHET

FALSE PROPHET

BY

STAN RICE

Alfred A. Knopf   New York   2003

THIS IS A BORZOI BOOK

PUBLISHED BY ALFRED A. KNOPF

Copyright © 2003 by the Estate of Stan Rice

www.randomhouse.com/knopf/poetry

Knopf, Borzoi Books, and the colophon are registered trademarks of
Random House, Inc.

Library of Congress Cataloging-in-Publication Data
Rice, Stan, 1942–2002
False prophet : poems / by Stan Rice. — 1st ed.
p.   cm.
ISBN 1-4000-4142-2
I. Title.
PS3568.I295F35 2003
811'.54—dc21
2003047415

Manufactured in the United States of America
First Edition

EDITOR'S NOTE

False Prophet is a collection of the last poems written by Stan Rice, who was diagnosed with brain cancer in August 2002 and died less than four months later. The whole sequence was composed between the end of July and the end of August 2001, and then revised in the months following. These pages preserve idiosyncrasies of spelling and punctuation that were characteristic of the poet, who in any case did not have the chance to correct the galley proofs of this book.

FALSE PROPHET

PSALM 151

Lord, hear me out.
At the point of our need
The storehouse shares its shambles.
We are calling to the heart
And desire information from place.
We call on the pain in the wicked.
They are prosperous, their footmen
Have wearied, their servants
Are swollen. But this is a walk in the park.
How are we going to keep up
With the coming floods. If we cant
Handle this we cant handle
The collar. Listen to this.
Listen to the straightforwardness of this.
Surely all day he has
Broken my bones in gall.
My leash he has caught in a hedge.
He lay as a bear pulled in pieces.
The arrows of his quiver have entered
My gravel. I have forgotten strength.
I have even forgotten about mercy.
Every morning I chisel a shadow
In springtime. Cheer my designs.
Provide me my desert to die in.
Great my might that erases
My heart. I cant make it past this.
My lamentations in winter and harvest
Have doomed to captivity my despised
Family. My looted father
Is chained to a wall in sewage.

But nobody's listening. Ive heard the weeping
Of the children as they were being
Cooked. But we can sing it.
Even if I am being scaled like a fish by you
I will not accuse you of my gloom.
I have an answer to that.
Our bellies are envious. We want it.
We want that promotion. We want
That pride. Their eyes are fat.
Therefore the riches increase
And are cast out in vain.
I would offend the fears
Of my mind if I struggled
With baloney. And I say no way.
Not a person alive I hope
Springs to his life but by
Lifting it up and claiming it.
The giant-killer paws the fair field.
I am chased by morning.
I am slippery.
                    Selah.

PSALM 152

Im tired of the fellowship of words,
The abundance of tradition.
Already it is wet outside
And my heart is a red stick
Beating a word.
My goal is impossible.
I am fully persuaded that staying-power
Is what keeps the true story alive.
It is what we do.
People began to sift through my lifestyle.
I came to know the backdrop against which
Mysteries happen covered with dirt.
There was dirt even on depth.
Eavesdroppers dwelled on my faults.
All by himself I was.
I walked with pagans.
I was one with anything grateful.
But I had no clue.
Feed me to the lions in the morning,
Then the body will be filled.
My life will be prayerless.
Then will the knowing come forth
As a reward for the subjective
And passionate. I long
But I dont know
My own heart.
Explosions feel good.
The pollen is enticed.
I am excited by heavenly places.
But listen.

How can we nail one hand
To the altar
Then go forth in the willingness
To be comfortable
And liked. We dont do
What needs to be done.
We dont see the miraculous because we need
Props. Like a tongue in its entirety
I long. Let the Red Lobster
Burn down, go to hell, in the earth,
Today. Some of us will be caught
A day late with a goat head
On our shining table.
But a dark spiral will
Eventually be made perfect
In our weakness. The enemy
I am running from is in
The midst of the enemy.
I was essentially hiding.
I woke out of my sleep
And put my stone pillow
Outdoors. If only
I had my own house.
This is not whining.
This is the dollar I am short.

Selah.

PSALM 153

I lay my head on a pillar
But was not prepared with a sacrifice.
Do you understand the distinction.
That's wonderful.
But there's a difference between seeing
And doing. A contrite heart
Walks uprightly growling.
I say this with love.
But dont admire me.
Be at my side.
Move with me.
See, we are waiting to be asked
To hold our breath.
Be prepared to move toward the problem.
Just this last Friday night
We opened the doors
And in came some ushers.
In the kingdom of places parts are a wave.
If you rush, the ferry will be on its way.
As will I.
      Selah.

PSALM 154

Is that old sock in the back yard
In a coffee can worth going to hell for.
Is a Superdome full of screaming women.
Im burdened for you.
I cant help it.
I havent been able to sleep all week,
Thinking about you who harden your necks.
All down the line my brain burned
As I pondered. How many times
Have you resisted the word
Then got cut off by a taxi.
Wroth, but to no avail. As
He who was stoned down to the last billy goat.
But he never listened.
His fingernails and toenails grew like the talons of the birds.
Listen now.
Are you going to have your way or bust.
Well then youll just have to bust. A raving
Message matters not to a jar.
Send the spirit of a fool to cry in the night.
On my heart lay terror.
We are not talking about the category of casual visitors.
A pointed man can sit
And wonder eternally. Day after day
You must pay the bills, but until you do that
You have been told.
Families have perished, have turned
And burned. Yet you have not heard
The soft-soap of flesh in the message.
Hell wont be hot enough to roast the both of us.

The smooth road gnashes its teeth.
In our living rooms, I tell you.
Your way will be washed of its will
Like a new creature. Someone
Will find you cold and blue in the bed
Some morning.
Itll be too late. Death wont
Wear off like aftershave. That's why
Butterflies like sweet water.
Im burdened for you.
I cant help it.
Listen now.
        Selah.

PSALM 155

An invisible government controls everything.
We dive right into a 43 year old truck driver.
The pizzas are wrapped in dynamite.
My wife and I got on the bulletproof bus.
No one knows for sure what tactic
Is disproportionate. Slowly, daily,
The dramatic is reduced. But the fantasy
Is the strategy. I can only
Speak for myself. Every result
Is the source of a third thing.
Historically input has its own head.
Its eyes are always the mob's.
Oil is murdered.
With the other hand roads are made smaller.
Theyre not going to drink it.
That's not the real threat.
On one pole is the agenda and on the other
There you sit.
Therefore they want a big war.
There is such bloodshed every throat
Is a fantasy. It's a paradox.
The theory is that the simple
Is exciting if the dialogue
Is the issue. The spiritual side
Prepares for the end of time.
Help those who are lost.
And their scribes.
                    Selah.

PSALM 156

I have arranged for the decades for months now.
Understanding presents its products.
No one wants to fight over violence.
Point-blank the priests hauled away
Thousands of tons of Mongols
And Turks. But here's what I want to know.
What does energy want of a ton of stone.
The cries are debatable.
The shield unites with the signs.
The schemes are protected by artifacts.
Remember the outcries from documents.
Outrages are sitting ducks.
It becomes legitimate to have half a brain,
Because the system is wound on a dagger.
The genius is that the human dimension
Is like two drunken fighters.
Im not too worried about the charge
Against seriousness. Over time
The enemy is reduced.
It is almost 1 a.m.
In five years we will believe in prophecy.
We are, indeed, like trumpets in crushed-velvet cases.

Selah.

PSALM 157

Who am I, Lord,
To harbor an impure book. Throw it away,
Into the garbage, hardback or paperback, even my own,
Rid myself of the half-committed,
Throw it directly into the plastic trash,
And then go on seeking the glass skeletons
Who wave flashlights and wear derby hats,
Whose acts emit more psyche than they ingest,
Whose ravings or whispers collect
And are the evidence.
                Selah.

PSALM 158

Each day I devoted to time.
Riches were radio to me,
And static the sound of rain on leaves.
Then I heard garbled voices.
Each selling a different deity.
Behind a brick wall people
Were torturing my honor.
Fires plagued my lakes and sea grasses.
I severed my ties with
The must-attend roof parties.
Skeleton crews chronicled
My plummeting remains.
Charity departed when I came aboard.
God knows I am flawed,
But a straightforward discourse
Is central to the long view of the Lord.

Selah.

PSALM 159

Government cannot be replaced
By the hounds that people may have.
But a powerful intellect is an easy target
And a double-edged sword brings great wisdom
To fewer than one in ten.
Education raises the web.
My shield, so far, is new people.
But hopefully next time
All things will not be cut in half.
Filmmakers will take a breath of fresh air.
Comedy and cocktails on Thursdays.
This is a new twist on scaffolding.
It begins at the top
And descends.
                    Selah.

PSALM 160

No teacher knows what works.
Theory after theory plays the marimbas in the lunchroom,
And olympic philandering
Sacrifices leadership on the lost.
Bells tumble.
Deposits cut down on calves.
Octaves are not what they were.
Then there's the gap
Under the wall of the rose.
What is the stuff of life.
An ashtray. A bowling shirt.
Finding things inside things.
                    Selah.

PSALM 161

I heard my first mandolin
On the victrola. Then my sister
Walked into the pasture
And was wed. Lord, why do you
Keep me on the phone until
I am deaf. There comes a day
When the mandolin must be put
In the mountains.
In search of a better life
Valleys inspire conflagrations in autumn.
Rosy the dirt is.
My heart lies down in it.
Im kind of speechless.
It takes my breath, the hammered dulcimer
Left out to be beaten by rain.
Can anything clothe the dreamstate
And keep the hopelessness in.
Have I heard my last mandolin.

                            Selah.

PSALM 162

May my joy spring forth
And break my heart like the flowering
Branches. No matter how bad it is
Let us stand. And the same day he said,
There rose a great storm
Among little ships. And he said
To the sea, Be still. While inland
The streams went whitely over the stones.
Do you really sense, as you walk around,
That it was a very hard day. Violet
Bridge over wide river looked like
A parable. I was exhausted.
And the same day evening came
From the other side. Reflections
Of rowboats wobbled. You cant see
The hills in the rain, the hills
We have just climbed to arrive at
This place among sheep and deer.
Beyond them, the seething gold of the ocean.
The trees as aroused as a cathedral.
Feeling no shame for their excess.
Maybe you have gotten on God's
Last nerve. May I be put
In the hinder part of the boat
On a pillow. The fish with flesh
As thick and white as bread,
May they spray forth from my heart
Like the petals of the cherry trees. May
I hear them, the bells of being,
Awake and asleep and between.
                              Selah.

PSALM 163

Soon I wont be able to think for myself.
I will only hear and obey the voices.
The radio alone will redeem me.
My face will be etched in the cave of life.
Consecrated airwaves will carry the cry
Of my errant life, yet they
Threaten to turn me from a creature
Into a thing. I lower my car window
And in sticks a horse its huge head.
Its eyes magnified by madness.
Will I regret my time alone in my room
Recording in ballpoint the ravings
Of the voices who keep asking me to call them
By phone but I wont.
Time allowing, I return to the conclusion.
No doubt my silence will get his attention.
I look for comparisons
And thereby am caught up in statements.
I am stripped bare of all parables
And my garments swept into a corner.
Brothers and sisters, I am
Not a swindler.
Stand and measure me.
My voice is increasingly
As true and as false as a song.
I look up at the black mesh of the radio speakers,
In which the fish are thrashing
Above and beyond the call.

Selah.

PSALM 164

I am humbled by this unmerited filthiness, Lord.
By my own depiction I am contrasted
To an angel standing some distance away.
Acute personification opposes me.
Even my eyelids were unworthy.
Like putty I lowered them.
I was broken, as usual. Wept
In brokenness. Up until that moment
Even atheists joined me.
And I was ashamed to be grieving.
The stench consumed me. The sorrow
Was in me like calories in chocolate.
Lord, this is between me and you,
As to which of us is the more depraved.
Am I your trained flea.
Can I be made free by sheer labor.
Then empty your chains at my feet.

Selah.

PSALM 165

I am weakened by my recovery,
Which is created from nothing.
Ten virgins came out of my radio
And turned off the spotlights on the iceberg.
My back was to the speakers.
They were a griddle of sound.
Originally happiness was easy.
Then I was punished by riches.
The devil has fled the details.
The force of law has divided the pie.
Order unravels. Over my head all is level
And I am in the crosshairs on my knees.
What can I do to distinguish between false hope and no hope.
The bushels fill up with schemes of plunder.
The buzz of nature at dark
Comes forward with the stroke of my pen.
What increases.
The nothing that everything comes from
And the everything that from it comes.

Selah.

PSALM 166

I have put myself in dark preserves,
The jelly of August. A rock crusher
Has rolled through the meadow.
A trashtruck has lifted me
And dumped me in and turned on
The compacter. My braver self
Stands at the mouth of every gutter
To see if I gush forth
Gleaming and smooth again. I
Reach down into the black jelly
Of my heart and hold out a handful.
It is part me, and partly the big teeth
And mad eyes of a horse.
                    Selah.

PSALM 167

Last week we were in Georgia, middle Georgia,
And people were scared of love.
Heels were upraised.
Judgment has been delayed. OK.
The world didnt end
Because so many people prayed
That it wouldnt so it didnt.
There is your proof.
Start fasting. Share humility. Watch a lot of TV.
Excitement is not information,
And if you dont like constant praising
You probably wont like heaven.
Let's go home.
There's no doubt love will stand up in the gap
From a wheelchair.
Even your job will be walking in the oven of God.
Advanced Prophetic Training
Will increase your safety.
The elite serial killers are among us.
Each micron is bent by judgment
And there's no time to put on a new roof.

Selah.

PSALM 168

Let me recap the case
Against mist surviving the bonfire.
Anti-attention will lead
To the desolation over and over
Again. Moonlight will melt
The olives. At midday
The trees will stand on their shadows
And then be darkened by rain.
Abominations will flee
Into the mountains. The field
Will be no bigger than your wallet
And meaningless to you.
Kingdoms will occupy
Each other with prophetic fulfillments.
Each thing will pertain to words.
Certain instructions arrived
At just the time
Shortwave radio caught up
With the moment. The great white throne
Had to change. We rearranged furniture.
Information has seven heads
And each of its heads seven eyes.
In the end, time will enrich
Every lesson. Including
"How long is one week," and "What beast."
The air is always current.
If you want to go deeper,
Rise.
　　　Selah.

PSALM 169

Two hundred million soldiers playing harps
Cannot sufficiently warn that a week is not seven days
When you are suffering yourself. It
Could be seven times anything.
Therefore we are out of the woods by anti-mathematics.
Once you know what that seven is
Remember to multiply by two. Time is
Butter. It wont take the veil.
So here we are again in the wilderness
With a demon divided into seven somethings
Multiplied by two
And added to level one.
How can the eyes of the evil
Be divided from those of the good.
By ear.
     Selah.

PSALM 170

The deceitful heart
Is captured and carried away.
It is forced to carry the king's cup
And the queen's neck-scarf.
I have a dangerous approach.
You owe it to yourself to focus
On calling me up. Weak
Is the lion in the river,
Feeble the saint in the mud.
It turns out that by cross-referencing prophecies
Everything is made clear in the newspapers.
To understand the puzzle
Break the parts smaller and publish.
It can change your marriage,
And an iron rod can give birth to a man-child.

Selah.

PSALM 171

The falling snow put out the brushfire.
A beautiful concept. But the melting snow
Triggered the mudslides.
I ate food and took drugs.
Severe muscle breakdown threatened.
I got a blood test. In tiny print
I found the full prophecy.
It predicted everything but itself.
A year's worth of wolves
Can cost thousands of dollars.
But the bush by the road burns for free.

Selah.

PSALM 172

I was in the province of shoeshine.
Current things gave me a picture.
The rocks purged rams.
Corn defeated the babble.
I was considering the whole.
A noble rage smote the ground.
Ego poked the beehive of the greater world.
The means were beastly. They fueled
The waxed turkey. They whacked
The small man. They dug a peace treaty
From the ground. The thorn in the side
Was reborn. The stars trampled themselves.
Many things cut my features in marble.
Hope was sacrificed and crashed down.
Truth prospered under the foot. The visions
Were in the hole. I stood afraid
And stared at my motionless shoes.

Selah.

PSALM 173

Sing your song financially in Rosedale.
Rays of light are talking about it.
And here it is, translated.
God's money is wise. And behind it
Enter the virgins in answer to the question,
What is this oil.
I am as anointed as a fish in the waters.
My yoke is destroyed.
My burden must slip from the oil.
Here is the parable.
I cant just take this suit off and live in rags and dig ditches.
In a tent or in a Holiday Inn riches are on your nose at the fore.
So he asked for a bowl of chill bumps.
I dont know what I mean.
I dont know whom to follow.
Who will lift up the hearts of those
Who constantly suffer themselves.
I dont know what is sung in Rosedale.
But the yoke is mental,
And the chill bumps pimple even the fish.

Selah.

PSALM 174

All my debt I consume and develop
As information and weapons.
This is talk at its best. All eyes
Are on the convoys at the border.
Across the street there is fire.
The windows bulge.
Extreme weather takes its toll even on vinyl.
I have sighted the skills to be mastered.
But dont worry.
I can play games with the bees
Disguised as a stick with aspirations
To cut the cheekbones of the bankers.
I will spend by a factor of three.
I have been burned by expansion.
In large part creation is fresh
And the dump is data
Howling to have its way
With the gash that reads as reflected light
In the pupils of marble statues.

                              Selah.

PSALM 175

I stared at my darling over the pillow
At morning. The Lord was with me.
Inches away was her open and startled eye.
Then I returned to my dream of the melting faces.
When I woke I wrote that time
Should be finished and shoved
Through the door, but it was too tall.
And the bride climbed the fig tree.
And the armies passed under her.
Even the thieves in the night
Did not hear her breathing
Nor the watchman behold her
In the darkness. The hours
Of darkness whisper their messages into bullhorns.
But lack of knowledge keeps the people asleep.
Our arms lie turned like wrestled creatures.
There is babble like in a birdhouse.
In sleep the mysteries are snakes
That in sunlight are thoughts of snakes.
And both are as carnal as the lioness
Whose shoulder blades rise and fall as she creeps.
The image expresses the eternal For Instance.
It is the likeness. It
Stares into the whale eye
Of the lover that rolls on the pillow.
                                        Selah.

PSALM 176

When I am appalled
By colossal artifice
The sad word
Is my fellow laborer.
What would make you
Want to forsake miracles
You are too close to.
Why.
My eyes are lights
In an emergency alert
System. The radio static
Sounds like water
Left on in the kitchen.
Not real silence. I
Am better off not having
Lived in the age of
Miracles for I can
Believe in them.
                    Selah.

PSALM 177

Everything that you can see out there with the natural eye
Is the first heaven.
This is a foretaste of the ghost.
Language cant pass from such smoke rings.
Therefore I hired a messenger.
He was a shadow reflected by a mirror onto a floor.
Believe it or not
People by the millions
Worship what walked on the earth.
But I could not realize it.
Compared to such pure light
Staring at the sun was peering at dimness.
The messenger was
A careful liar. But I had a plan.
And we went over Obedience Falls.
We were dots, we were invisible from an airplane.
I saw patterns where others saw chaos.
My natural eyes were a bucket of golf balls
And a golfer showed me the light.
                              Selah.

PSALM 178

Join us as time ends. The mysteries
Must be talked about.
Concerning the parable of the judgment
There has been much controversy
Between the sheep and the goats.
They all were virgins, so they were not being accused
Of partying or stealing the oil.
Some people have no talent for servitude.
They would swindle a cheeseburger.
There are different criteria for judgment
From different angles.
The coattails lead to the key.
Pretend that you don't agree with me,
Then you will not be taken unawares
When the left-handed goats
Are divided from the glorified sheep.
If you are adjudged trumpeter trumpet for them.
If you feed lambs only meat they will starve.
But they will grow fat on praise.
So the sheep end up owning the kingdom
And therefore clearly the sheep are the winners.
And the goats? They will eat even
The book.
      Selah.

PSALM 179

Several hummingbirds came down to polish my shoes.
They, too, were virgins with oil.
But you cannot go to paradise
Without distortion by death.
It's not professional but it's true.
If a piano player buries his hands in the yard
He will experience a weird darkness
That will be crystal clear to the sheep.
For they are strangers to everybody.
What if suddenly there were no goats,
And in seeking them a thief plunged into a ditch.
He was loaded. But who was
The neighbor of this man.
Let's face it.
The mysteries are how things should be
Not how they are.
The sheep are often too busy
To find a life in the ground.
But the goats leap up to eat the prophecies
And each stone unturned turns itself.

Selah.

PSALM 180

I walked through the woods at night blindfolded
So I would not fear the dark.
Then the ghosts were set on fire
Because they had walked past a naked stranger.
Time made me choke up.
I shared your words with my fellow inmates.
I was in prison and you visited against my grain.
So many people get tangled up
In sacrificing dead people to perception.
The bees give and the bees receive.
But there's something about ground meat
That inspires us. Be ready to do good
To the content.
For the evil eat bread also
And after the walk the blindfold is always wet.

Selah.

PSALM 181

From translating the radio voices
My hand is weary. The thumb
Has pushed. The little finger is sticky.
All month I have been the scribe of the sinning angels.
But this is a joy to live through.
For who can put into words the twinkling of a trumpet.
I am the servant who did not bury his hands.
Passages pass.
The goats frighten the sheep and the sheep
Frighten the deer and the deer
Frighten not even the fireflies. All this is commentary.
The lightning flashes on honesty.
A lot of people hold that view.
But the ink comes out constantly.
Until the hand
Is a rack of lamb.
                Selah.

PSALM 182

I came seeking honey
But found the hive deserted
And maggots eating
The orphaned larvae.
It was a biblical image
Of the overly sensual in hell.
This I can assure you is impersonal.
Maggots come to the windows
To see what all the commotion is about
On the street. The cycles are passing.
Sweet, sweet.
        Selah.

PSALM 183

The Lord's estrogens come not
From the urine of a pregnant horse.
Leeches in coffee soften.
A woman's body is enhanced water.
Daily their intake of themselves is great.
They lack the mental clarity of cruelty.
So the bones are lost in the blood.
Here comes the queen with the lamb in her arms.
The horses rot like the soldiers.
The storehouse is simply the day.

Selah.

PSALM 184

I who am damaged need a clean slate
And a plan. Turn me
Into good news.
The crusade that ends in hugs
Continues as speaking tours.
In answer to your question
The spirit is always busy.
And we have powerful dreams,
Very accurate and specific
About particulars you can check out in the news.
Fighter jets flew from a turkey.
Its rear waxed over.
Then the prophets lit up
By being grafted together. Keen was the cry of the post.
All soft arms rush to the aid of intelligence.
And the godless are as forgotten as flies
Though they make a noise like the sea.

Selah.

PSALM 185

You will stand on the brink
And see fools eating worms in the morning.
You will see prophecy videotaped.
You will quote the enemies of the soul
And tell jokes to the same so-called God.
Before loving your enemy you must stand on his harp.
Everything will be updated
Each time the sun ovulates.
All of this is just a suggestion from the omnipotent.
Why debate over minutiae
And make naked your necks to the sword.
Why turn your back on the roots.

Selah.

PSALM 186

The invisible man is straining to get through the knot hole.
Eat warm spirit and weep.
Become as pink-faced as the gorge of the tulip.
Reality has turned the drying lime shoe polish brown.
Ladies and gentlemen Im not making this up.
Eight hundred million people are in our living room.
Now ancient history
Is three months old.
How many males must be slaughtered
To put out the fire on the back burner.
A pizza shop explodes in my kitchen
And yet all the eggs are unbroken,
For they were as words in the memory.
The only place of safety
Is in this bulletin.
Do you think you know what it means.
So did they.
       Selah.

PSALM 187

The Lord makes me reborn on video.
Crush time and you get a rubbery powder.
The fighting cocks are all chained to their stakes.
We are dealing with people's heads here.
Frankly when I sat down I frightened even myself.
But something is wrong with this statement.
The database may itself be a hate crime.
The preachers chill me. Anointings congeal
En route to the cornfield.
I hope Im not overdoing this.
But that is what this is about.
Something is against whitewashing beheadings.
Is that taking it too far.
Even tribulation is free speech.
Even anti-batter makes the fried chicken crisp.
No matter what your prophecy is
You must swim until your skin is a robe.

Selah.

PSALM 188

In the arms of neighbors
Nestles the hair of the back of the neck.
Rise and walk through the principles.
Do they make sense.
All of a sudden the millennium is behind us.
Here come the beasts again.
Fireworks in daylight are just yellow smoke.
Hideous. The drooling cow
Is a psychic. The rooster also
Has powers. We cant even figure out how we got here.
But if we dont do it
Who will be cruel enough.
Nobody, if the end comes before the dot.
My phone is vibrating and my neck is stretched
And my neighbors are as faceless as fryers.

Selah.

PSALM 189

After the war everyone was shorter.
Two sources are not necessary
To confirm
Mind-control.
The scales scream to be cleansed.
So history brought them in, clean as a rabbit.
The book I refer to is granite with sources.
It isnt just ink on paper.
The Lord is exactly one year old.
I know. I have combed his hair.
His murmuring is the sound of his listening.
Who killed John Kennedy?
No one you know.
                    Selah.

PSALM 190

I was a chef on the Lord's battleship.
It was foul, it was slavery. Radios
Played only the organ.
Repeating things was the only proof they were true.
The horned ones hobnobbed with prophets.
Lines were thrown out to those listening.
We were alive and jumped up
As we spoke. The trial was the fourth thing.
It perfected us. Divers tested our work.
The hardest thing to do is wait.
Delays endure in spite of our trust.
I was as patient as a scalpel
But still I had pain in my fill-in-the-blank.
What am I doing wrong.
A kitchen knife on the Lord's battleship
Healed my daughter and son.
Trials are not sins.
The pain is gone, the pain is gone.

Selah.

PSALM 191

Three days in the deep I searched for my heart.
The way was without detours. Surely
Something wants to discourage me
From intimacy. Am I going through something
Or is something going through me.
My appointment to suffer is canceled.
Im smelted and snapped.
My priorities once again cause me to rely on the joy
Of the scourge. I cast my torment on the fire.
Once again, the tape and the title are one.

Selah.

PSALM 192

For a week now I have been going from door to door
Looking for a witness to my father's world.
The spheres go silent. Still waters
Submit to abuse. Rust presses its taste on the leaf.
Forgetfulness battles with the hush of the wind.
I sought the original web and listened to the sisters
Whispering to the entities.
My conscience was rained on
By soldiers in goggles.
Door to door I went,
Fearing the system.
At death the marriage is no longer binding,
And the angel's fists fall from its wrists.

                                 Selah.

PSALM 193

People stood up in steam and touched me.
Without tantrums I would have no mission.
The brain seeks specific forms
From the sources of focus.
But I was from Texas and as a result
My valuable time was no problem.
The minimum energy was sufficient to father the word.
The Lord is all natural and easy to swallow.
Welcome back to TV and marriage.
We are all in the same boat
And under our skins move the oars.

Selah.

PSALM 194

My staff is real, from the head on down.
Nobody paid me to wear this armor.
A boy birthed out of form
Crossed the barriers of youth.
I was anointed by giving up.
Gravity pulls the ghosts' tongues.
Juice comes from the earth,
But Im not that pure. The world
Flows most purely through the newest hose.
Let this boy touch your chains.
Let them slip. The rest of the week
Let your waiter serve you two fleshes,
First to one foot and then to the other.
Your rock and your shield face the Devil.
It's not a strange thing that you are a sissy in armor.
Take up your face. When youre sick
Take up your magnified stripes
And show them.
Voodoo, hoodoo, you do, I do. The darkness
Can be quenched before it takes root in the helmet.
Now Im as hard as a cow.
You cant go to a casino just to eat good food.
Sooner or later that garbage
Will enter the heart, then babies, and ultimately comes morning
And the sword that is in your head
Is so bright you can shave in it.
                              Selah.

PSALM 195

One day I ate a sinner.
From solid ground a dog took my hand.
I was pulled from my brother.
He howled in victory.
I thanked him for being poured from the riches.
Do you have desires for packages.
Of course you do. I shine like a bride.
My garments are designed to attend
The drama of the scenery and the creatures.
Pride of the bone earns
Expulsion from the absolute. Sea-doves
Nest in the tree of life. Immediately
The cool voice of the garden hid itself.
He was naked after he had put down his glove.
An angel prevented splendor
From coming up from the seeds.
Hold forth especially the beans
And fold up for the Lord.
No matter how warm the prison
The only posture is that of
The lover. Lore
Leaves a stain
Unlike other fictions. You have read
Of the elder morons of today, the butchers.
Their guts make a bucket of a jar.
Why am I complete
But for the idea of nearing the forward point
Of so much bunk that it calls for light.
They are not moved by volume,
But the saints made like you most of the time

Rise from the pillows of hell
Out of shame for their burning birthplace.
A sensitive person is dumbstruck
By the visualization of anybody
Sitting in a current of coals.
Walking down D Street this is so.
100 degrees below zero you will stand
Like starched laundry for nothing.
Your suit will be buried without you.
Some folks try their best to burst early.
Some are buckled to the pulpit
So they cannot thrust.
All night the road sets itself
Apart from the pedestal. The voice must
Be face to face with woe.
Tiny hands must seize my lifestyle.
I am not fit to be in the presence of pain.
I know I have a previous image.
Some of us look at our brothers and sisters
And descend to the grove of the dove.
Can you stand in the coal mine with the Lord.
The Lord takes a man bare
To the law. His handiwork is his witness.
When they got to the graves
They were worn out. The poles had cleaned themselves.
The mountainside pulled off their shoes.
They broke clean from the quick
Then came to the baby's side.
Enemies were in our nest molting.
Our hose soaked the room.
I saw him the way he is.
The exalted see urine as it is.
I had a good ear for wings.

On my route I was all alone.
Two ways led through the rubber hose.
I saw the candle cry.
I saw myself as I was. And when I cried out
I was glad to be in unison with the mild.
My witnesses are the cold dead,
But I'd kill myself
Before reading their names to mere bones.

                                        Selah.

PSALM 196

On the sabbath I heard our dead pastor's voice
On the subject of obstacles.
He said the bones could be refreshed
And letters could be sent to those
Who stood in the breach and whined.
I am tired of walking in mist.
The obstacles stand in my house.
I have seen their faces in the barbershop or in Wal-Mart
But their souls are as unknown to me
As the cattle.
God doesnt work through many.
Let me put my finger on this darkness.
When I do, sin enters me like a sliver.
I hurled the word and I shortened my hand and
My face cried into the searchlight.
How long has it been since someone cried out
In your office, I am lost! I am lost!
Did it refresh you.
Were you more poor, or more proud.
How long do you seek the face
Of nothing short of a broken heart. Utterly,
The blame takes the curse, the curse
The sorrow.
           Selah.

PSALM 197

Every fifteen minutes
The lost mash a mansion
And sweeten a lion's den
With love. Lift the spirit
And show it as linen.
Showers call to our house
To have mercy. But the motive
Mostly is victory. If you pray
Mercy will flower from silver,
And gold from the glove.
I have tried other patterns
And blamed the cheeseburger's blood
But my wonder came due
When I was washed of time.
Deception turned to me
In my desire and fainted
In the harvest. The laborers
Had compassion on me
And listened carefully
To my message. After which
I lost my job and
The world had no pity
On pity.
       Selah.

PSALM 198

At the sound of the works my love compares
To the promise of nothing. Strong hairs
Throng to the egg yolk. People have horses
In the sunshine. Should we be afraid
Of the turning point. The coming night
Cannot be escaped. I am following
The horse with somebody to write with.
Cannon are heard in the clouds.
I open my heart. My eyes harmonize. The message
Says someone will ride in on an anti-horse.
I came to the wheat and the oil.
My life cost a penny.
Famine was a spot on a sphere.
Starved out and hurt was the beast from the hair.
The stomach cast a white shadow.
Then I threw a family of six into my garbage can.
My dog ate better than they.
Long lines gleamed before us moving toward empty.
Again the horses hated us, for we had the keys
To what they are. In dozens of pale green frames
Death leads the swords to drink.
For the tenth time my songs are drenched
In the drippings of plague. Prophecy
Overtakes the majority. Prostitutes
Bring blood home to the wives of doctors.
One hundred times greater
Is the infection of the world than the book.
Are you afraid of the verge.
There are beasts that carry disease are there not.
Let me tell you something about rats.

Rats carry fleas as their beasts.
The divine has an order in keeping
With privacy, but the horses of order
Are sorrowful because this is just
The beginning. Nobody I love
Can go through that. Past which
Each of us goes out of here flaming.
What will happen we cannot make up.
Save me from the wrath of love.
Touch me each day with the sword of
The egg, of the dishwasher, of the authentic.

                                        Selah.

PSALM 199

My enemy is elastic. His camp has a front and a back.
He is the chief of hiding.
His identity can hide in salt. His wiles
Are the sisters of knots. I put my
Deep water port in his campfire
And my stem in his path.
His speech will have no idea.
He will freeze in his tent
And sit on a cone until clarified.
He will think my words when he thinks of himself,
And by his own tongue be unmanned.

Selah.

PSALM 200

The lowered bait lit up my study.
But my surplus was small, so I consented
To be fed lead.
We read, we enrich
The hairy, we are recipients of rain.
Though I am high in the language
And therefore tending toward silence
From here to the horizon
There is nothing but whispering and violence.

Selah.

PSALM 201

By short-wave the prophet
Pushes the witness through the dark in a wagon
To the dream of the end.
You will see the knowledge fill the world as the waters.
Words at any given time seduce evil from wax
And peril shall magnify its time in the proud.
Incontinent heads and lovers of jobs shall
Turn away from being part of the day when
If it were possible the elect shall write letters
That touch my heart. The time-line is proceeding,
And loosed from the new moon is the rejoicing
Of forests, and messages rage in each need of
The pine needles. More clearly each day
The body teems with miracles. Satan's long orange tongue
Touches people in good health. But the Lord
Has a question. Is binding and loosening the same.
Physical branches fast in heaven but on earth
Heaven loosens the names from the patterns.
I repented, and listened, and was embarrassed by war.
I was held over hell and shaken.
Brothers battle each other and my wife speaks against me
And the blood is standing up like a tree
In a gown. After the changing I nonetheless
Rushed into life. I pondered my cursing.
It lasted for about four days. Then I was 16.
I was up in the radio room.
As I am while alive to inform you.
                                        Selah.

PSALM 202

I am in position to fear the present.
I need to hear from my enemy. My eyes
Are a ghost's. I try to figure out
What is screaming in my ear. I feel dumb
And lack strength to write
What is apart from me.
I cant solve the life pumping in deep places.
I have lain my brain
In the laughing lice.
So I just stand here stupidly enjoying my life
While dismay belongs to the stretching Lord
In his bondage as his bark floats by.
                              Selah.

PSALM 203

Many more sank than went out
On the waters. Listen to this solo
Sorrow, into whose arms
You have fallen. Stand on its face,
And be overcome by the chorus
That covers your chains
With its whispers. Stay still
As the presence breathes
On your crisp hairs.
Take hold of each and savor it.
The voice lies down beside you.
The mid-day richness forecasts your path
To the deadline of future death.
When you are lonely, listen.
Selah.

PSALM 204

Lord, a voice from a loudspeaker said each night,
If you intend to hang yourself
Put a piece of paper with your name on it in your mouth
So we will know who you are.
Who are these martyrs as folded and pleated
As roses. Questions dwell on the earth
But the murderers are still talking.
No doubt judgment will blind us in our fullness.
This is the voice of the air. It comes in small scale
To turn again on the neck.
It saves two witnesses from the silence.
Reprobates will eat words with nobody home
And people will be jerked from this world like puppets
And the price will be trust in faith with their lives.
The fire will be cut off and die in the silver.
A voice from a loudspeaker will say nothing
And the spirit will operate again as a torturer.
A bloodbath will draw nigh.
Even worse than the last.
And those who are interested in prophecy
Will notice there is none. And think of
The fury of the children of so-called ministers.
It is intellectually passé to think goodness is bad.
Salvation and destruction fornicate in the rafters.
Down comes the sun-shaft of dust.
Without hatred,
How could it not.
                    Selah.

PSALM 205

I have enjoyed the dark-roast of six decades. Now
My canary whets his beak on his sandpaper perch incessantly.
I have experienced the icy feet and the tingling hands
Of madness, and I have
Rolled my eyes as the eighteen oaks were cut down,
And in brief I was on the brink of the pit.
And who was
The mastermind of the scenario in which I
Found myself locked with my ignorant
Bliss. I make salary. I go to the mall. I make salary.
I go to the mall. I continue flying. I do not perish.
The terrorists are busy. That's what they want.
The line returns to the point. I
To my songs.
       Selah.

PSALM 206

Satan has two characters. One
Marches children across minefields.
The other has an embargo on him.
Only well-placed bribes
Can clarify the economics of bribery.
I know this because
In my previous life I was a liquid.
There are so many weep-holes in my conspiracy theory
That no single conspiracy can flourish.
So.
I was flying to Orlando.
In the seat across the aisle was the Lord.
He had a long brown stinger.
I began to realize the extent of the exterior.
Did you know their army is starving.
Their hands are out.
Corruption eats at the certain.
You say there is neither conspiracy nor corruption.
All Im saying is that the airplanes are crashing,
And Satan has two characters,
And the spirit is in the mail.
                              Selah.

PSALM 207

Our pruning hooks were not ready.
Prophecy shook the orange trees.
Down they plopped in the bloodbath.
Be not troubled for what must need be.
Your warhead might be squeezed.
Your arms might increase to sixteen.
Nameless is the color of the tea in the afternoon light.
So far we are unrecognizable.
I looked up and saw the scattered anti-clouds gather.
And I pulled the hooks
From my jaws, and the unshielded tea
Was stained red. But I was not alone,
For yesterday it was prophesied
That the daily news was evidence of
The harmony among all things, also called
Resolved stress. Lord, I am not ready to be so blown away.
My orange trees dont fruit because rats
Eat their flowers and my heart is food
For the air.
       Selah.

PSALM 208

My yoke chaps my shoulders. I have stopped thinking
In circles.
That was two years ago.
By force white paper issues from fear of forms.
And here we sit.
Thunder without lightning.
The watermelon colored crape myrtle flowers
Melting each afternoon.
Sweeping up arms from the marble floors. Putting them
In gift baskets. I am blameless
But the lightning is no respecter of persons.
In prophecy nothing is irony.
The Lord is on the brilliant ball balanced.
Conspiracy is obvious in the patterns in the plywood,
And the plowed fields seen from an airplane
Make Satan gnash at his chains.

Selah.

PSALM 209

For two weeks I have been listening
To the radio prophets quoting me.
I have flopped in the words like a fish on the bottom of a boat.
Great vines embrace themselves lovelessly
And the hedges look poured from a mold.
Nothing can contradict the logic of prophecy
For it follows the methods and forms of the roots.
I am parting the words from their utterance.
Through the translucent mass moves the light,
And the veins of the rose petals are magnified,
And we gaze in astonishment at the core of the core
For its hunger is the hunching of the heart.

Selah.

PSALM 210

The core comes last, as silent as a violin
In a safe. The unblown trombone lengthens and shortens,
Gold showing oiled silver
Then darkening it.
The trumpets inhale. All things visible
On the core cluster and glisten
Like ants on a lemon drop.
The prophecies meet and are sealed in the ink.
A log falls from my eye, a lion from each ear.
I dont want you to miss this.
I love this.
The best part is the fertility of the symbols. I laugh
At their literalizations. They fill the brain with interpretations
Like molecules of a gas fill a room.
And the soul gets as firm as a balloon.

Selah.

PSALM 211

My ongoing study of prophecy
Arrives at the book where the lamb that was slain
Turns over its dead face and ogles me.
My eyes open in wonder.
I paw the toilet briefly.
Unspeakable words should be studied together.
To understand I must remember
The picture before me of the lamb's skin
Full of blue lightning bolts which were the veins
In which the blood had stopped moving.
In the scene there's a book
And in the book there's a hand.
And someday that hand will slip into my pocket and squeeze.
But for now I sit staring
At the pulsing scroll.
My will is worthless to alter the front or the back.
Once again the scholars are raving
About riddles. Rest never comes.
Lightning without thunder illuminates the corpse of the lamb.
Suddenly all prophecies are vile.
Lies and platitudes.
Even the butchers know this.
Even the smoothed sheet knows.

Selah.

PSALM 212

Why think these songs irrational.
They are no more so than the hive.
In mercury I seek the method of the molten.
I remember mercy in my praise of the chain.
The green apple is red where slapped.
Why should my psalms sicken, or be blasted
Like blackbirds by shotguns from trees.
Why would you bypass being adored by the radio.
For each gift pump the moment.
The herring are numerous
And the Lord's sperm are words,
As am I. I was lost
And sang my broken-down songs in the hell of the hour.
Then in my heart moved an oar,
And I was found by a breeze from a door in the sea of forms
And was rowed to the cherry trees on the shore.

Selah. Selah.

A NOTE ABOUT THE AUTHOR

Stan Rice (1942–2002) was the author of seven previous collections of poetry, including *Red to the Rind* and *The Radiance of Pigs*. For many years he was a professor at San Francisco State University. He received the Edgar Allan Poe Award of the Academy of American Poets, the Joseph Henry Jackson Award, and a fellowship from the National Endowment for the Arts. Rice, who was also a painter, was a longtime resident of New Orleans, where he lived with his wife, the novelist Anne Rice, and their son, the novelist Christopher Rice.

A NOTE ABOUT THE TYPE

The text of this book was set in Electra, a typeface designed by W. A. Dwiggins (1880–1956). This face cannot be classified as either modern or old style. It is not based on any historical model, nor does it echo any particular period or style. It avoids the extreme contrasts between thick and thin elements that mark most modern faces, and it attempts to give a feeling of fluidity, power, and speed.

Composed by Creative Graphics, Allentown, Pennsylvania
Printed and bound by United Book Press, Baltimore, Maryland
Designed by Peter A. Andersen